A Love Letter to the Anxious Brain

Namrata D'souza

BookLeaf Publishing

India | USA | UK

Presentation by *BookLeaf Publishing*

Web: www.bookleafpub.com

E-mail: info@bookleafpub.com

ISBN: 9789363313187

First edition 2024

ACKNOWLEDGEMENT

To my soul sister, a writer I admire, and editor, Mitchelle Rozario Jansen. God knew what He was doing when we became friends in college. To Meryl, my September friend and editor, I will always love you. To my dear and ridiculously talented friend, Madonna Rozario Jansen, thank you for writing your book of poetry, Echoes of My Existence, and inspiring and pushing me to write this book. Your words are magic, as you know.

To my biggest cheerleaders, who believe I can win the world if I set out to do so – Surbhi, Ameya, Gauri, Pareesha, Noyonika, Rajeshwari. They say it's dysfunctional to find family at workplaces, but I am blessed to have found people who match my freak (I apologise on behalf of the millennial community for adopting this Gen Z phrase).

Hi, I am Alice – Part I

Hi, I am Alice.
Did the author
introduce me in the preface?
Probably not. Probably for the best.

She likes naming things, this one.
I wasn't always called Alice.
But calling me so makes her happy.
We allow that. She needs it from time to time.

You could say I am a furry little creature.
Monsters Inc. takes after me. I should charge
royalties.
Tiny feet left naked so I can creep up on the
author.
Big, doleful eyes that cry every time

My scissor-sharp tongue cuts her open.
I don't mean to. You must believe me.
If it was up to me, she'd live in my windowless
room forever. (who needs to dream?)

No, I know. You think I am clever. I really am.

My intelligence is my downfall.

It's all in my head

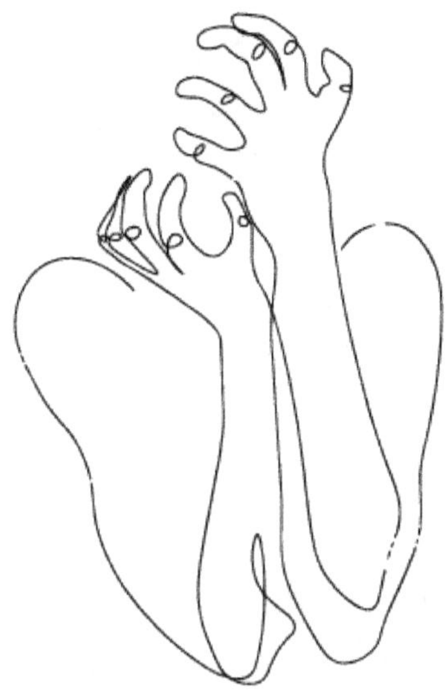

Your poetry follows
A precise meter.
A rhyme scheme.
Measured in syllables.
It's structured.
Conforming.

I need to write
Poetry by arranging
It symmetrically
Across the page.

I allow my words
To only take up
So much space
On a line so as to
Look pretty and I
Call this madness
Poetic liberty.

Go on, tilt your
Head to the right.
Can't you see the
Skyline I built?
Words stacked
As buildings;
Not too tall
Not too short
Just about right.

Just about right.

I only take up so
Much space in
The world as it
Would look pretty.
Hair done well,
Lips painted red,
Tattooed hands,
Eyes fierce,
Smile confident,

Demands lesser,
Weight petit,
Breasts tighter,
Hips lighter.

Just about right.

Do you want to
See what happens
When the illusion lifts?

Iamnotenoughiamnotenoughiamnotenoughiamn
otenough

Look, the symmetry's off.
Well, it's all in my head, anyway.

How's the heart doing?

It is okay.

These three words, they do not
shatter the earth beneath your
feet, when they arrive.

No thunderclaps in the sky
No booming waves
crashing on the banks;
a sign of good things to come.

Where's the show?
Where's the fanfare?

These three words do

not impress a suitor, no.
No grand gesture, they hold.

These three words simply
exist in one spoken breath.
inhale it is / *exhale* okay

How's the heart doing now?

It is okay is to simply be.
It is okay is bravery whispering
in your ear.

What if I fail?
inhale *it is* / *exhale* *okay*

What if I disappoint people?
inhale *it is* / *exhale* *okay*

What if I am not the person I made others
believe I am?
inhale *it is* / *exhale* *okay*

What if I am not the person I thought I was?
inhale *it is* / *exhale* *okay*

What if I am not good enough?
inhale *it is* / *exhale* *okay*
inhale *i am* / *exhale* *enough*

Mountain Girl

She
She walks
Walks with a mountain
Mountain inside her heart
Heart that's battle-worn
Battle-worn and stripped
Stripped to near rubble
Rubble and dust
Dust from which she rose
Rose to fight
Fight and love
Love who she was
Was and is
Is me.

She is me.

Why I live

I got words hidden
under my nails;
sewn into the lining
of my coat,
tangled in my hair,
playing hide-and-seek
with the colours on my lips.

I got words dancing
on my fingertips,
racing along the
sides of my heart,
raging in my pits.

I got words
trekking along
the length of my skirt,
peeking from my boots,
sketching art along
the scars on my back.

I got words
And so, I live.

Summer

For someone who doesn't particularly like the
heat, I often daydream about Summer.

Brown curls framing a face that
I term uncharacteristically enthusiastic.
"Can you stop smiling for a second, Summer?
That's not natural, you know," I'd scold.

He wore shirts so crisp, the break of dawn
was in fact Summer stretching his arms.
He'd laugh a mouthful of sunshine

every time I mentioned this to him.
"My silly Winter love," he'd call out to me,
his hands reaching out as cherry blossom
branches.

Summer is who I wish to be.

Popsicle kisses

Would you call me crazy
if I say blue tastes
like popsicles
made of mountain shards?

That when I bite into blue
a thousand icy splinters
pierce my tongue
and what bubbles forth is
I love you.

Kissing you is blue.

A recovering perfectionist's prayer

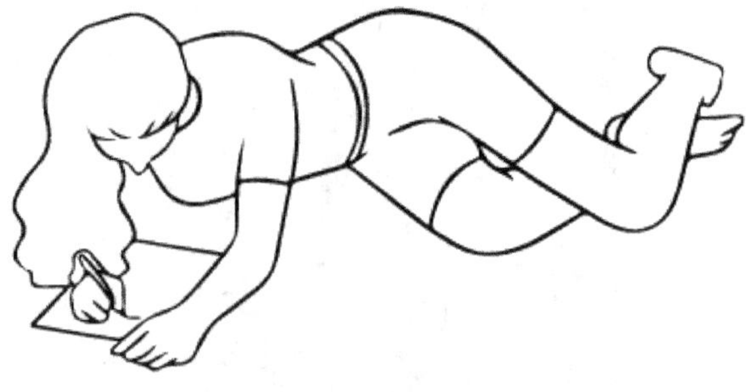

Thank you for this new day.
Thank you for the roof
above my head.
Thank you for
my mother,
my brothers,
and my friends.

Please let it be a good day.
Please let me not make any mistakes.

Thank you for the blessings
bestowed and luxuries gifted.
Thank you for the food I eat,
and the water I drink.

Please let me not make any mistakes.
Please let everything go well today.

Thank you for the work I do;
for the doors you've opened
and the dreams that've come true.

Please let everything go well today.
Please let me not disappoint anyone today.

Thank you for this life.

Please let me not disappoint anyone today.
Please let me make you proud.

Hi, I am Alice – Part II

Do you remember me?
You met me a few verses and pages ago.
Probably not. Probably for the best.

Unlike the author, you have a choice
to not take me and my forebodings seriously.
Unlike the author, I cannot find a space
in your palms or feet and sing my songs.
She calls it tremblings; I call it lullabies.

A flick of your fingers in my direction
and I promise I will run. Flight is my specialty.

You see, I love this one. She... doesn't.
I get it; I am not the kindest, but
I have been with her since she was all but seven.

She is all I have.

The price paid

The sea and I meet
at midnight to exchange few
secrets untold; drown.

Spat out by the sea,
the land holds space for my dreams.
To earth, I return.

When I hug the sky,
I remember the price paid;
new body, old soul.

Last Woman Standing

I'd like to think I have a large heart.

How else would you explain
all of these tiny beating vessels
resting in my palms, my feet, my gut?

Tiny hearts split from a single
device scattered all over my body.

My personal landmines
that detonate at the
slightest whisper of anxiety.

"Alice, was that you?"

My body is a recovering war zone.

I am the last woman standing.

Lay down your weapons, friend

"You are a fighter. Not a quitter."
I wore this as a badge of honour.

Fighter. Warrior. Soldier.
Fighter. Warrior. Soldier.
Fighter. Warrior. Soldier.

My words of affirmation,
my daily prayer.

Pretty proverbs covering cracks.

Lay down your weapons, friend.
Lay down your weapons, brain.
Sit back, put your feet up.

Breathe. Breathe. Breathe.

The fight lasted years.
Take a break. Take a goddamn break.

Monsters under the bed

Eight letters each,
monsters and memories.
We can't put this down to
language being funny.

Bring them out now, come on.
Cajole them into life once again.
Under the bed is still under your skin
And that's no place for them to live.

I've brewed a pot of tea for four
Invited myself to this party, if you please.
Sit yourself down now and remind them,
this body isn't theirs to have and hold.

What was ravaged at seven, against your will,
has been rebuilt from the ashes;
you have loved it into existence, you reign
supreme.

Ask them to pack their bags,
their sooty fingers, ragged breath, et al.
Leave. LEAVE.

This is my home. My temple.

A Love Letter to the Anxious Brain

If I were to describe myself in sunflower years,
I'd probably say my Tuscan sun yellows are
giving way to warmer tones of marmalade and
ginger.
The freshness of spring no longer marks my
countenance.

I've stopped following the sun. Resigned myself
to accept crumbs of light rather than turn my
face and bathe in it.

But why? Oh, why did I stop following the sun?

Whose word made it bible that said we were too old to drown in sunshine? Come out and play, oh dear heart of mine. Play with warmth and touch and all your spots and marks and softness. You're not too old to feel giddy, impossibly in love. Your roots are stronger now. You are stronger now.

Turn your face towards it.
Follow the sun.

Let
Love
Find
You.

Remember who you are

I am the daughter of
the moon and sky.
I am stardust come alive.
I am magic written into
existence by the Divine.
I am earth renewed.

Falling in love at 34

I know, that title isn't reassuring.
I know, I am swatting fear like flies.
I know, I should be wiser, braver.
I know, I must speak my heart.
I know, I must open myself to love.
I know, if I don't, why am I living?
I know, that if you love me too,
Life, as I know, will change irrevocably.
I know, that if you love me too,
I may never stop smiling, even in our fights.
I know, that if you love me too,
I will believe in fairy tales.

I don't know if I believe in fairy tales.
I don't know if I believe I deserve it all.

I know, 34 feels no different than 16.

Bucket List

That when I cross paths with a mirror
I won't squeeze the rolls of my body into
submission.
Breathe, child, breathe. Gently.
Take space, child. L O U D L Y.

That I won't let the Impostor sneak in
through the door left ajar
every time I welcome Success.
That I will drown
its voice out

with my song.

That I won't let labels
signed off by society
define my worth.

That I won't hesitate to
use my voice for revolution,
won't press pause
if there's no audience.
That I know words are magic
And will find their destination.

That I won't shut the door on love;
won't pack away my vulnerability
into a fear-filled trunk.
That I will befriend love.
Beginning with the person in the mirror.

To Alice

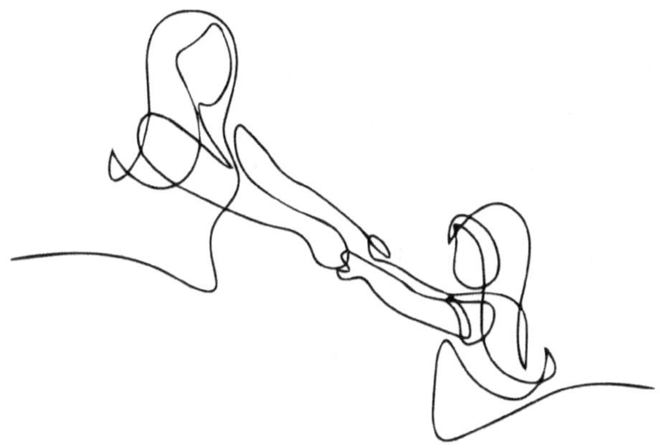

Dear Alice,

Let me introduce myself to you. I am she, the author.
The one who loves naming humans, animals, objects, and mental disorders alike.

You are me, Alice. And I have known you like I know myself.
You can stop cowering near (within) my feet.
Come along, sit with me, won't you?

You are me, Alice. I have hated you up until some years ago.
What changed? I wanted to test if you respond better to love.

Plain and simple.

You do.

You are me, Alice. But I, the author, am so much
more than my anxiety.
Let's shake hands on that, Alice.

Thank you, I love you.